YOUR KNOWLEDGE HAS VALUE

- We will publish your bachelor's and master's thesis, essays and papers

- Your own eBook and book - sold worldwide in all relevant shops

- Earn money with each sale

Upload your text at www.GRIN.com
and publish for free

Bibliographic information published by the German National Library:

The German National Library lists this publication in the National Bibliography; detailed bibliographic data are available on the Internet at http://dnb.dnb.de .

This book is copyright material and must not be copied, reproduced, transferred, distributed, leased, licensed or publicly performed or used in any way except as specifically permitted in writing by the publishers, as allowed under the terms and conditions under which it was purchased or as strictly permitted by applicable copyright law. Any unauthorized distribution or use of this text may be a direct infringement of the author s and publisher s rights and those responsible may be liable in law accordingly.

Imprint:

Copyright © 2018 GRIN Verlag
Print and binding: Books on Demand GmbH, Norderstedt Germany
ISBN: 9783668947306

This book at GRIN:

https://www.grin.com/document/480684

Philipp Schlander

Blockchain And New Economic Paradigms

GRIN Verlag

GRIN - Your knowledge has value

Since its foundation in 1998, GRIN has specialized in publishing academic texts by students, college teachers and other academics as e-book and printed book. The website www.grin.com is an ideal platform for presenting term papers, final papers, scientific essays, dissertations and specialist books.

Visit us on the internet:

http://www.grin.com/

http://www.facebook.com/grincom

http://www.twitter.com/grin_com

Blockchain and new economic paradigms

Seminar Report

Goethe University Frankfurt
Chair of Law and Finance
Frankfurt am Main

by
Philipp Schlander

P2P Finance
Summer Term 2018

List of Figures

Figure 1:   Paradigm Shift..5

Table of Contents

1 Introduction 4
2 Blockchain Overview 4
    2.1 Distributed Power 4
    2.2 Paradigm Shift 5
    2.3 Benefits of blockchain 6
        2.3.1 Cost Efficiency: 6
        2.3.2 Transparency & Trust: 7
        2.3.3 Immutability: 7
        2.3.4 Security: 7
        2.3.5 Time efficiency: 8
3. Sample Use Cases on blockchain 8
4. Blockchain as a catallaxy 10
5. Conclusion: 11
Bibliography 13

1 Introduction

During the past years arising technologies and globalization have forced institutions and companies dealing within different challenges of digitalization. Systems and applications have become more complex and interconnected, setting a difficult problem for the current legacy systems and applications.

With the invention of Bitcoin in 2008 by a person or group of people known by pseudonym "Satoshi Nakamoto", a solution to the challenges of globalization and digitalization was introduced to the world (Bashir 2018). Not Bitcoin as a cryptocurrency by itself, but the system Bitcoin is based on: blockchain technique. This new technology promises to radically alter the existing paradigms of nearly all industries including IT, finance, government, media, medical, energy and law as the most important ones (Bashir 2018, p. 8). The topic of this seminar paper is to elaborate the revolutionary implications of blockchain on different sectors and to glance at possible future aspects of blockchain's potentials setting a new paradigm.

2 Blockchain Overview

So what is blockchain all about? Let us have a look at the key elements and why this is likely to become a game changer.

2.1 Distributed Power

Blockchain is a public decentralized ledger platform (Evans 2014). Across a peer-to-peer network, it distributes power with no single point of control (Tapscott 2018, p. 33) and can simplify the current paradigm which is the disparate nature of the systems. Blockchain reduces the complexity of managing separate systems because as a distributed ledger where information is updated automatically, it can be used by all parties during the same time.

Consequently, keeping lots of separate systems up to date and synchronized between each other is not needed due to the concurrent use of the same ledger with the same information. This implicates that blockchain structures disorganized systems which makes them significantly more efficient and incorruptible, because no centralized version of this information exists for hackers to corrupt. The revolutionary effect of such a distributed ledger can be applied to disrupt any centralized system that coordinates valuable information (Wright and De Filippi 2015).

2.2 Paradigm Shift

Blockchain is a disruptive, innovative technology (Swan 2015; Wiles 2015; Pilkington 2016) whose core benefit and service is providing decentralization (Bashir 2018, p.42). This general service of blockchain will lead to a paradigm shift from the current paradigm of centralized systems to the new paradigm of decentralization as shown in figure 1. Combined with the objective of working out the paradigm shift, figure 1 is applied, which presents a transaction example between two parties.

Figure 1: Paradigm Shift

Current paradigm: reliance on a third-party intermediary

First party   First party bank   Intermediaries   Second party bank   Second party

New paradigm: no third-party intermediary, reliance on blockchain

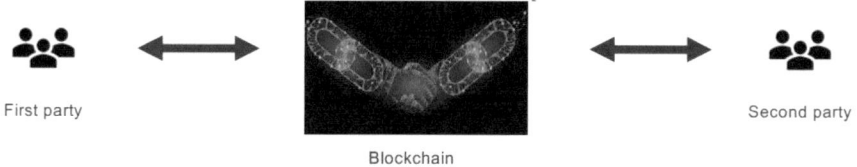

First party   Second party

Blockchain

1 Source: https://www.feflogx.de/bezahlmoeglichkeiten/, 18.06.2018
2 Source: https://www.tibco.com/blog/2018/02/05/enterprise-blockchain-how-is-this-different-from-bitcoin-technology-use-case-comparison/, 18.06.2018

The most efficient structure to create, establish and enforce rules is centralization at the beginning which minimizes duplication and implements clear hierarchy (Davidson, De Filippi, & Potts 2016). The current paradigm is the reliance on a third-party intermediary like PayPal, Visa or Mastercard. There is no possibility for two parties of acting directly with each other because central systems like banks and intermediaries are placed between. In the current paradigm intermediaries are a necessary entity because of their responsibility of transferring money from one bank to another bank. Banks are also essential because they provide the movement and production of capital and the operation of the payments system. They can be seen as a centralized ledger of transactions matching savers with borrowers and intermediating on two sides of the market.

Blockchain is about to disrupt this intermediation by matching two parties directly which leads to the new paradigm. It is characterized in the redundancy of a trusted third party and in the reliance on blockchain for peer-to-peer or business-to-business transactions. Enabled by blockchain as a peer-to-peer electronic cash system based on cryptographic proof instead of trust, any two willing parties can directly transact with each other (Catalini & Gans 2017, p.1). Conceptually it is possible of placing blockchains alongside markets, as an open platform technology performing this decentralization service (Potts 2001). According to Vitalik Buterin, blockchains as decentralized systems are converging on being a 'world computer' (Wood 2015) meaning the idea that any application running on such a platform will be global in reach.

Because of this new decentralized opportunity through technological enablement, there are a lot of options and benefits through Blockchain which will be explained in the next abstract.

2.3 Benefits of blockchain

In order to work out the future predictions and impacts of blockchain, it is significant to address the most important advantages of blockchain technology at first. The main benefits are (2.3.1) cost efficiency, (2.3.2) trust and transparency, (2.3.3) immutability, (2.3.4) security and (2.3.5) time efficiency.

2.3.1 Cost Efficiency:

Intermediaries have a substantial market power because their advance in knowledge allows them to charge up fees for their transaction service. Same time they gather further power by having unique and rich access to transaction data between market players. Inefficiency, reduced innovations, the presence of a single point of failure, privacy risk and censorship risk are the consequences of these mark-ups (Catalini & Gans 2017, p.16).

Blockchain facilitates costless verification by allowing peer-to-peer and business-to-business transactions to be completed without the need for a third party. Having no third party, the transaction costs converge against zero. Furthermore, the costs of centralization rise the more they become vulnerable to exploitation while the costs of decentralization fall due to technological progress (Davidson, De Filippi, & Potts 2016, p. 5). As a distributed ledger blockchain becomes "increasingly cost effective to centralized solutions as they run down three exponential cost curves: (1) Moore's law (cost of processing digital information, i.e. speed, halves every 18 months); (2)

Kryder's law (cost of storing digital information, i.e. memory, halves every 12 months); (3) Nielsen's law (cost of shipping digital information, i.e. bandwidth, halves every 24 months) (Wiles 2015)" (cf. Davidson, De Filippi, & Potts 2016, page 3). Due to the strong learning curve of technology, blockchain is driving to a technological substitution against the mature technology of a centralized ledger (Davidson, De Filippi, & Potts 2016, p. 3).

2.3.2 Transparency & Trust:

Blockchain is also a trustless technology, meaning that instead of requiring a third party verification, it "uses a powerful consensus mechanism with cryptoeconomic incentives to verify authenticity of a transaction in the database" (cf. Davidson, De Filippi, & Potts 2016, p.3). Blockchain has an open-source structure which offers users a complete control over all the information and transactions stored in the distributed ledger. Enabling every member making a change in a public blockchain and viewing all changes that are made. Because of this, a perfect transparent system is created and as a result of transparency, trust is established. So "trust in the intermediary is replaced with trust in the underlying code and consensus rules" (cf. Catalini & Gans 2017, p.8).

2.3.3 Immutability:

Immutability of Blockchain describes the extreme difficulty of changing information maintained in the blockchain. The transactions are placed in a chronological chain-order and as more blocks are added during time, it becomes more difficult to tamper. A bad actor would have to spend a disproportionate amount of resources to change past transaction data because he would have to outpace the growth rate of the legitimate chain and to recompute all blocks after the manipulated block as the blockchain network is always taking the longest, valid chain as the true state of the ledger (Catalini & Gans 2017, p. A-2). Therefore, information in blockchain systems cannot be changed, modified or lost which provides a permanent historical incorruptible record.

2.3.4 Security:

Before being linked to the previous block, every single transaction is automatically validated and cryptographically secured by the blockchain. Furthermore, information is stored across the decentralize network rather than on a single computer, making it tough for hackers accessing it. Blockchain allows a privacy-preserving way of verifying transactions through preventing information leakage by allowing market participants to verify transaction attributes and enforce contracts without exposing the underlying information to a third party (Catalini & Gans 2017, p.6). The private data problem is removed due to the redundancy of exposing private information to a third party intermediary and the safety of private data not being reused of the original contractual arrangement (Catalini & Gans 2017, p.6).

2.3.5 Time efficiency:

A further major benefit in adaption of blockchain is time efficiency. Analyzing traditional transactions, usually it takes days to settle completely, it requires a third-party intermediary and is prone to human error. Blockchain can automate and make this process faster. Any data inputted into the blockchain is transmitted and stored automatically, so in real time. Cutting out intermediaries, there are also less transactions to absolve. Furthermore, blockchain is working 24 hours a day seven days a week instead of traditional banks having some services during business hours five days a week only.

3. Sample Use Cases on blockchain

Integrating blockchain technology into business is about shifting the common approach of centralization and addressing the organizational and business challenges of digitalization through a standard peer-to-peer or business-to-business architecture. This challenge is being faced by Hyperledger.

Hyperledger is a cross-industry collaboration founded by the Linux Foundation in December 2015. It includes companies ranging from the IT sector to the mobility technology sector over financial industries to blockchain start-ups such as Daimler, IBM, JP Morgan and Blockstream. Hyperledger is not just a single blockchain. It is a platform for blockchain based solutions and provides a framework for companies to build up their own blockchain relying on smart contracts. One of the first applications on Hyperledger is Rdw.

Rdw is a road transport initiative and it has developed a blockchain solution for bicycles in the Netherlands. The concept behind Rdw is that information about the bicycle are being saved in the blockchain and most important the ownership. This means that for example if a theft occurs the bicycle can be tracked via GPS-chips allocated to the blockchain and it can clearly be specified to whom the bicycle belongs, police can easily see and check whether a bicycle was locked, register the theft, transmit the claim with the insurances which in turn can trigger payment, all in a closed and trusted environment, almost in real time. Before, this has been a cumbersome process lasting weeks, if not months.

Here, blockchain works as a proof of ownership. It creates a transparent, resilient and efficient distributed ledger (Davidson, De Filippi, & Potts 2016, p. 3). Trust in the intermediary, here the owner, is not needed anymore because it is replaced by trust in the blockchain technology. The blockchain in that sense can be called trustless. But this technology can not only be applied to bicycles, it is applicable to all cases where information is required to be publicly validated (Davidson, De Filippi, & Potts 2016, p. 18). It can "represent ownership in currency, intellectual property, equity, information, contracts, financial and physical assets "(Catalini & Gans 2017, p. 3).

Another possible application of the blockchain technology is politics where blockchain can be used to introduce a crypto-democracy. The trust in the voting institutions can be raised and the costs be lowered to a more efficient use of democracy such as public referenda. Democracy can reach a more efficient scale by its transnational charac- teristic.

Blockchain technology affects multiple industries, is borderless and has an impact already now. Currently, it is mostly applied in the telecom, insurance and financial services industry. These sectors are becoming more engaged mainly by having huge cost pressures and their resulting focus on process efficiency, supply chain and logistic opportunities. But still most companies are conservative to invest into the blockchain (Furlonger & Kandaswamy 2018). This occurs because the blockchain technology is currently overhyped. There is huge visibility and media coverage of blockchain providers represents a different blockchain as it is available currently. It can be expected that upcoming regulatory landscape will reduce the speed with which the blockchain technology is growing. Cryptocurrency laws to date are not standardized and confusing. There is no consistency between country regulations. The same is true for accounting and taxation treatment. Additionally, the scalability of blockchain technology is still a problem. Blockchain currently is still too complex for mainstream adaption. Most blockchain applications are still in the early phase and main stream adaption is only supposed to be in the next ten years. Companies will find ways to standardize blockchain applications and are motivated by the first-mover advantage.

4. Blockchain as a catallaxy

Blockchain can also be seen as a catallaxy. Following Hayek "a catallaxy is a special kind of spontaneous order produced by the market by people acting within the rules of the law of property, tort and contract" (cf. Hayek 1982, p. 109). Catallaxies do not share a common interest, they consist "of a number of individual objectives, which no one knows in their totality" (Hayek 1988). The agents living in this order follow their own plans.

Blockchains can be seen as catallaxies creating their own economies. They coordinate distributed groups of people and compete with the current organizations. Furthermore, they reduce the size and scale of effective catallaxies through the above outlined five benefits.

With having a better flow and an improved coordination of knowledge, wealth is created.

In centralized organizations trust is necessary, as the intermediaries have the possibility of rent-seeking. But trust can be exploited, i.e. by using the data that intermediaries get hold of and can use. Some of today's highest valued companies such as Google, Facebook and Amazon exploit exactly this. This problem does not occur in decentralized systems such as the blockchain because trust can be produced crypto- graphically. Efficiency is being created by eliminating the rent-seeking possibilities in centralized institutions. The elimination of rent-seeking leads to a competition between centralized organizations and blockchain technology which will lead to an interplay called cryptosecession (MacDonald 2015). Agents can now exit the incumbent institutions. As a result the possibilities of rent-seeking will be reduced.

Let us have a look at cryptosecession in banks. We are not looking at blockchain technology being adopted, blockchain is to be seen as a competitor and or replacement to current systems here. Agents do not have to stay in the exploiting mechanism of the banking and money system. This means that the overtaxing proclivities of banks have to be cut back (De Filippi 2014). Banks have to pay respect to the wide range of applications of entrepreneurs and businesses operating on the cryptosecession frontier (Stigler 1971). The development in blockchain technologies and applications allow a successful cryptosecession. One instrument for cryptosecession are cryptocurrencies as they „permit citizens to escape the circumstances of 'optimal monetary exploitation´ "(cf. Davidson, De Filippi, & Potts 2016, p. 9).

But it does not only compete with incumbent hierarchical institutions such as a central bank but also with legacy banking, financial organizations and markets "(Davidson, De Filippi, & Potts 2016, p. 9).

5. Conclusion:

As a conclusion from the previous considerations it can be drawn that blockchain technology has a great innovative and disruptive potential and can be seen as an institutional or social decentralized technology for coordinating people (Davidson, De Filippi, & Potts 2016, p.1). Because of Blockchain there will be a paradigm shift from the current paradigm of centralized systems to the new paradigm of decentralization. Blockchain technology promises questioning already existing processes up to the development of completely new business models without the need of third part intermediaries. It enables for example the automatically buying and selling of renewable energy generated by neighborhood microgrids in Brooklyn (Breuer 2018).

There are two possible approaches of blockchain changing current economic paradigms. The first economic perspective describes the adoption of blockchain technology by current organizations in order to establish their sustainability. The second one focuses on blockchain as a technology of decentralization and therefore understand it as a new institutional technology competing with central systems like organizations and markets (Davidson, De Filippi, & Potts 2016, p.18). Evolutionary discovery is enabled by such institutional competition. Both will play a key role going forward.

As Blockchain is still new, it has several challenges to overcome. Key challenges include uniforming standards as a prerequisite for cooperation across country, sector and company boundaries and the current lacking scalability which means that blockchain is simply too complex for mainstream adoption unless it can be packaged up in a more user-friendly way. In addition, legal foundations and security aspects are essential factors for the blockchain to establish itself. The Hyperledger project is a key example of standardizing the application and to allow successfully and more easily integrating blockchain across the value chain like it has been exemplified in the use case from RDW.

Summing up the discussion, it can be concluded that blockchain technology will have a fundamental impact on different sectors, though it will take some more years until it become really mainstream, also because the new technology presents numerous challenges. One of the early sectors where the disruptive potential will be unleased is the financial sector which is characterized by high cost pressure, needs in efficiencies and further acts as an intermediary. Blockchain's impact on the global market is still in its infancy, but could quickly pick up speed. The World Economic Forum estimates that by 2015, ten percent of global gross domestic product will be processed by blockchains (Leichsenring 2017).

To finalize, we are still at the beginning of this new technology and nobody can foresee the exact full consequences blockchain will have but it is sure that it will have a fundamental impact.

Bibliography

Bashir, I. (2018), 'Mastering Blockchain', Birmingham, Packt Publishing

Breuer, H. (2018), 'A Microgrid Grows in Brooklyn', [online] available at: https://www.siemens.com/innovation/en/home/pictures-of-the-future/energy-and-efficiency/smart-grids-and-energy-storage-microgrid-in-brooklyn.html (28.06.2018).

Catalini, C. & Gans, J. (2017), ′Some Simple Economics of the Blockchain′, Massachusetts, [online] available at: https://papers.ssrn.com/sol3/papers.cfm?abstract_id=2874598

Davidson, S., De Filippi, P., & Potts, J. (2016) 'Economics of blockchain', [online] available at: http://ssrn.com/abstract=2744751

De Filippi, P. (2014), 'Bitcoin: a regulatory nightmare to a libertarian dream', Internet Policy Review, 2(2): 1–11

De Filippi, P (2014), 'Bitcoin: a regulatory nightmare to a libertarian dream', Internet Policy Review, 3. Online at: http://policyreview.info/articles/analysis/bitcoin regulatorynightmarelibertarian-dream.

Evans D. (2014), 'Economic aspects of Bitcoin and other decentralized public-ledger currency platforms' Coase-Sandor Institute for Law and Economics working paper #685.

Franco P. (2015), 'Understanding bitoin' ,Chichester, Wiley

Furlonger D. & Kandaswamy R. (2018), ′Blockchain Status 2018: Market Adoption Reality′, [online] available at: https://www.gartner.com/doc/3869693/blockchain-status--market-adoption

Guo, Y. & Liang, C. (2016), 'Blockchain application and outlook in the banking industry', [online] available at: https://link.springer.com/content/pdf/10.1186%2Fs40854-016-0034-9.pdf

Hayek, F. A. (1982), 'Law, Legislation and Liberty: A New Statement of the Liberal Principles of Justice and Political Economy', Routledge

Hayek, F. A. (1988), 'The Fatal Conceit: The Errors of Socialism', Routledge

Hyperledger (2018) , [online] available at: https://www.hyperledger.org, downloaded on 19.06.2018

MacDonald, T., Darcy Allen & Potts, J. (2016), 'Blockchain and the Boundaries of

Self-Organized Economies: Predictions for the Future of Banking', Melbourne, [online] available at: https://papers.ssrn.com/sol3/papers.cfm?abstract_id=2749514

MacDonald, T. (2015), 'Spontaneous Order in the Formation of Non-Territorial Political Jurisdictions' ´, [online] available at: http://ssrn.com/abstract=2661250

Milne, A. & Parboteeah, P. (2016), 'The Business Models and Economics of Peer-to-Peer Lending', [online] available at: https://www.ceps.eu/system/files/ECRI%20RR17%20P2P%20Lending.pdf

Leichsenring, H. (2017), 'Neue Geschäftsmodelle durch Blockchain-Technologie', [online] available at: https://www.der-bank-blog.de/neue-geschaeftsmodelle-blockchain/studien/technologie-finance/26816/

Peltzman, S. (1976), 'Toward a more general theory of regulation', Journal of Law & Economics, 2: 211–240

Pilkington, M., (2016) 'Blockchain Technology: Principles and Applications' in F.X. Olleros and M. Zhegu. (eds) Research Handbook on Digital Transformations, Edward Elgar. [online] available at: http://ssrn.com/abstract=2662660

Potts, J. (2001), 'Knowledge and markets', Journal of Evolutionary economics, 11(4): 413431

Rdw (2018), [online] available at: https://www.rdw.nl/over-rdw, downloaded on 19.06.2018

Stigler, G. J. (1971), 'The theory of economic regulation', The Bell Journal of Economics and Management Science, 2: 3-21

Swan, M. (2015) 'Blockchain: Blueprint for a New Economy', O'Reilly Media: Sebastopol.

Tasca, P., Liu, S. & Hayes, A. (2016), 'The Evolution of the Bitcoin Economy: Extracting and Analyzing the Network of Payment Relationships', [online] available at: https://papers.ssrn.com/sol3/papers.cfm?abstract_id=2808762

Topscott D, Topscott A (2018), 'Blockchain Revolution' New York, Portfolio/Penguin

Wiles N (2015) 'The radical potential of blockchain technology', [online] available at: https://www.youtube.com/watch?v=JMT0xwmFKIY

Wood, G. (2015), 'Ethereum: a secure decentralized generalized transaction ledger' http://gavwood.com/Paper.pdf

Wright, A., De Filippi, P. (2015) 'Decentralized Blockchain Technology and the Rise of Lex Cryptographia' SSRN: http://ssrn.com/abstract=2580664

YOUR KNOWLEDGE HAS VALUE

- We will publish your bachelor's and master's thesis, essays and papers

- Your own eBook and book -
  sold worldwide in all relevant shops

- Earn money with each sale

Upload your text at www.GRIN.com
and publish for free